THE ASBURY PARK PRESS PRESENTS

SANDY

THE JERSEY SHORE IN THE EYE OF THE STORM

APP.com ASBURY PARK PRESS

THE PRESS

A GANNETT COMPANY

ACKNOWLEDGMENTS

Thomas M. Donovan, President and Publisher, New Jersey Press Media
Hollis R. Towns, VP/News, New Jersey Press Media
James Flachsenhaar, Managing Director, Content and Audience Development, New Jersey Press Media
James J. Connolly, Multi-Media Editor, New Jersey Press Media
Magdeline Bassett, Assistant Multi-Media Editor, New Jersey Press Media
Karen Guarasi, Regional VP/Advertising and Marketing, New Jersey Press Media
Regina Longo, Regional Marketing Manager, New Jersey Press Media

Staff photographers:
Peter Ackerman
Robert Bielk
Tanya Breen
Thomas Costello
Mary Frank
Douglas Hood
Thomas Spader
Mark Sullivan
Jason Towlen
Robert Ward

Special thanks to:
Ann Hayes
Alyssa Calderone

FOREWORD

Slammed with winds gusting at 89 mph and soaked by a foot of rain and a storm surge of 8½ feet, the Jersey Shore never stood a chance.

As it crept up the East Coast, superstorm Sandy had already snapped off fishing piers, pushed trees through buildings and reshaped the coasts of North Carolina, Virginia, Maryland and Delaware – all from hundreds of miles offshore.

Then, on the evening of Monday, October 29, 2012 the 900-mile wide behemoth – fueled by warm Atlantic Ocean waters and supercharged by a western snowstorm – crash-landed on the New Jersey coast near Atlantic City.

Although none of New Jersey was spared, Ocean and Monmouth counties bore the full brunt. Boardwalks went missing. Boats were smashed, sunk and tossed into houses. More than 2,500 light poles were snapped.

An unrelenting storm surge destroyed houses and businesses, buried cars, and damaged or destroyed the Shore's protective dunes. By the time the storm eased on Tuesday, thousands of us were swamped, thousands more homeless. So much for our carefully constructed defenses.

Nearly 3 million New Jerseyans lost power, many for more than two weeks. And in parts of some coastal communities, including Ortley Beach, Lavallette, Mantoloking, Sea Bright, Union Beach, Point Pleasant and Seaside Heights, it wasn't clear when power – and people – would return.

For the Asbury Park Press, telling the story of superstorm Sandy has been a full-time endeavor. We have interviewed more than a thousand victims, rescuers, and officials. In helicopters and on foot, we captured videos and images of breathtaking devastation. Sadly, we reported on the deaths of more than three dozen New Jerseyans, including at least five in Monmouth and Ocean counties.

We would be forgiven for picking up and moving inland but – already – we are planning not only to rebuild, but to do so in smarter and safer ways.

This book, the first of two we shall produce on superstorm Sandy and its aftermath, benchmarks the storm-wrought destruction. In early 2013, a definitive book will tell the fuller story of Sandy, the Jersey Shore and our determination to rebuild.

Profits from both books will be donated to the American Red Cross Jersey Coast Chapter and the Jersey Shore Convention and Visitors Bureau.

Thomas Donovan

Thomas M. Donovan,
President/Publisher
New Jersey Press Media

OCT. 28 - 9:26 AM | Curious residents stand on the lookout at Holgate watching the approaching storm while geotubes designed to help protect the beaches are already taking a battering from the waves. This section of Holgate went out to sea in the storm. PHOTO BY PETER ACKERMAN

OCT. 28 - 10:49 AM | A boarded-up post office on Ocean Avenue in Sea Bright reminds people that no matter what the weather, the post office is still open, as preparations were underway for mandatory evacuations in Sea Bright due to approaching superstorm Sandy. PHOTO BY MARY FRANK

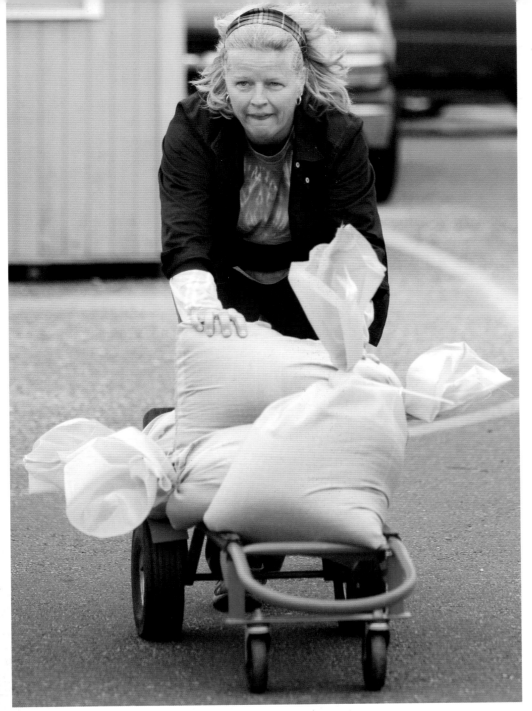

ABOVE | OCT. 28 - 12:08 PM | Karen Rosenberg, of Brick Township, takes a snapshot of the message on a home along the boardwalk in Point Pleasant Beach. An intense surf is hitting the Jersey Shore ahead of the storm. PHOTO BY TOM COSTELLO

LEFT | OCT. 28 - 12:19 PM | Linda Walton, of Belford, owner of the Riverfront Restaurant in Sea Bright, carts away bags of sand in preparation for approaching superstorm Sandy. PHOTO BY MARY FRANK

FAR LEFT | OCT. 28 - 11:28 AM | Paul Maniscalco of the Point Pleasant Beach Police Department goes door to door informing residents of the mandatory evacuation. Maniscalco talks with Seymour Avenue resident Debbie Harris, who will not be evacuating, but staying in her home to ride out the storm. PHOTO BY TOM SPADER

ABOVE | OCT. 28 - 11:42 AM | A treasure hunter using a metal detector scans the eroding beach in Point Pleasant Beach as Sandy's waves begin to pound the beach. PHOTO BY TOM SPADER

RIGHT | OCT. 28 - 11:51 AM | Chris Surgent, of Manasquan, and his sons Charlie, 15, and Will, 10, get their boat out of the water at the Deep Creek Cove Marina in Manasquan as Sandy approaches. PHOTO BY BOB BIELK

FAR RIGHT | OCT. 28 - 12:21 PM | Bill and Larisa Ippolito fill sandbags on the beach in Manasquan. Their home is near the beach and vulnerable to flooding. PHOTO BY BOB BIELK

OCT. 28 - 6:49 PM | Jenna Hetem, 15, of Atlantic Highlands, runs from the crashing waves on a jetty in Sea Bright as superstorm Sandy begins her descent on the Jersey Shore. PHOTO BY MARY FRANK

OCT. 29 - 9:27 AM | Waves crash over a wall at the end of Plaza Court in Long Branch as Sandy bears down on the Jersey Shore. PHOTO BY MARY FRANK

ABOVE | OCT. 29 - 8:45 AM | A JCP&L worker tends to downed power lines on a fallen telephone pole along Comstock Street in Asbury Park. PHOTO BY MARY FRANK

LEFT | OCT. 29 - 10:45 AM | Charline Myers and Jamie Gowan, both of Highlands, row a raft along the flooded Waterwitch Avenue in Highlands. PHOTO BY TANYA BREEN

BELOW | OCT. 29 - 10:23 AM | A van plows through floodwaters on Route 36 W in Long Branch. PHOTO BY MARY FRANK

OCT. 29 - 11:00 AM | A passing bicyclist stops to photograph a flooded car stuck on Baltimore Avenue in Point Pleasant Beach. PHOTO BY TOM SPADER

OCT. 29 - 11:05 AM | Dan Deviny, of Highlands, evacuates his 5th Street residence with his dogs, Congo and Deisel, through flooded Miller Street. PHOTO BY TANYA BREEN

OCT. 29 | Lisa and Dan O'Hara's East Avenue home is shown in the center of this image taken Monday afternoon as heavy surf from superstorm Sandy washes over the dunes in Bay Head. All that was left of the home after the storm was pilings in the sand. PHOTO BY TOM COSTELLO

OCT. 29 - 2:12 PM | Chris Wojcik, Point Pleasant Borough, holds onto his hat as he visits the oceanfront at the end of Bridge Avenue in Bay Head. Rough surf is battering the Jersey Shore ahead of superstorm Sandy. PHOTO BY TOM COSTELLO

ABOVE | OCT. 29 - 4:25 PM | Barbara Jeffrey of the Parkertown section of Little Egg Harbor Township, gets her three small dogs settled in for the night in the Animal Shelter set up alongside the evacuation center at Pinelands Junior High School in Tuckerton. PHOTO BY PETER ACKERMAN

RIGHT | OCT. 29 - 12:35 PM | Kayakers paddle past a utility truck along Elizabeth Street in South River in the hours prior to the landfall of superstorm Sandy. PHOTO BY JASON TOWLEN

OCT. 30 - 7:06 AM | Edison firefighters battle a house fire with live wires down on Heathcote Avenue in the early morning hours after Sandy struck. PHOTO BY JASON TOWLEN

ABOVE | OCT. 30 | People walk through debris at the Paradise Park community of mobile homes in Highlands. PHOTO BY TOM COSTELLO

LEFT | OCT. 30 - 9:52 AM | Peter Teresi, of Woodbridge, shows a kitten he found while looking though boats that were washed ashore in the parking lot of the Perth Amboy Yacht Club. Teresi plans on keeping the kitten and naming her Sandy after the storm that caused all the damage to the Perth Amboy waterfront. PHOTO BY MARK R. SULLIVAN

FAR LEFT | OCT. 30 - 8:31 AM | High tides forced boats out of their moorings and onto the shore line of Cheesequake Creek just below the Garden State Parkway in Old Bridge Township. PHOTO BY MARK R. SULLIVAN

ABOVE | OCT. 30 - 9:42 AM | Jay Santos (blue jacket) helps the Ballis family evacuate their home in the Cherry Quay neighborhood in Brick Township. They are John and Sueann in the boat at left and daughter Christie behind Santos. PHOTO BY TOM COSTELLO

OPPOSITE | OCT. 30 - 9:33 AM | A Perth Amboy firefighter walks near the badly damaged waterfront in the aftermath of superstorm Sandy. PHOTO BY JASON TOWLEN

ABOVE | OCT. 30 - 10:10 AM | A passerby observes the destruction to the King of All Cars Used Car dealership in Asbury Park after Sandy tore the roof off the building. PHOTO BY MARY FRANK

LEFT | OCT. 30 - 10:03 AM | A street light dangles from a snapped telephone pole on Heck Street in Asbury Park. PHOTO BY MARY FRANK

FAR LEFT | OCT. 30 - 9:59 AM | Union Beach sergeant Timothy Kelly looks at a Prospect Avenue home which was knocked off its foundation and destroyed. PHOTO BY TANYA BREEN

ABOVE | OCT. 30 - 10:22 AM | Union Beach sergeant Charles Ervin and Union Beach patrolman Shawn Gilkison assist (middle) Union Beach patrolman Robert Harriott retrieve essentials from Harriott's sister's Prospect Avenue home, which was severely damaged. PHOTO BY TANYA BREEN

LEFT | OCT. 30 - 11:57 AM | Frank Castrogiovanni, of Woodbridge, walks along Route 9 South in Woodbridge carrying empty gas cans to try and fill them at a Wawa Service Station. Power outages caused long lines at the gas pumps following superstorm Sandy. PHOTO BY MARK R. SULLIVAN

OPPOSITE | OCT. 30 - 10:13 AM | Union Beach sergeant Timothy Kelly looks at a Brook Avenue home, which was knocked off its foundation and destroyed. PHOTO BY TANYA BREEN

OCT. 30 - 1:08 PM | A local resident looks over the aftermath of a house explosion along Noe Street in Carteret that burned three homes to the ground. The family in the residence had just been rescued from rising flood waters from the storm. PHOTO BY MARK R. SULLIVAN

OCT. 30 - 3:06 PM | Bob Hofmann, of Verona, and his daughter, 16-year-old Courtney, leave Beach Haven West of Stafford Township with some valuables along with other residents after checking on their second home. Flooding was bad especially in the homes nearest the bay. PHOTO BY PETER ACKERMAN

OCT. 31 – 7:44 AM | Bumper cars pushed out of the Skooter building at the Keansburg Amusement Park area after Sandy. **PHOTO BY TANYA BREEN**

OCT. 31 - 7:57 AM | Arcade games, bumper cars and game prizes riddle Beachway in the Keansburg
Amusement Park. PHOTO BY TANYA BREEN

OCT. 31 | A car wedged under a house and buried in the sand in the Holgate section of Long Beach Township. **PHOTO BY ROBERT WARD**

OCT. 31 | Damage from superstorm Sandy on Long Beach Island. PHOTO BY ROBERT WARD

ABOVE | OCT. 31 | A bulldozer clears debris off Route 35 at North Street in Bay Head. PHOTO BY TOM COSTELLO

RIGHT | OCT. 31 | Trailers strewn about at the Long Beach Island Trailer Park in Holgate, a section of Long Beach Township. PHOTO BY ROBERT WARD

FAR RIGHT | OCT. 31 | Long Beach Township Mayor Joeseph Mancini talks about damage to his town, with a house that was washed of its foundation in the background. PHOTO BY ROBERT WARD

ABOVE | OCT. 31 – 11:39 AM | National Guard members help to unload evacuees after rescuing them from the Barrier Island. PHOTO BY DOUG HOOD

LEFT AND FAR LEFT | OCT. 31 – 11:23 AM | Shoppers converge at Wegman's on Highway 35 in Ocean Township to stock up on necessities after the store reopened its doors following the storm. PHOTO BY MARY FRANK

ABOVE AND RIGHT | OCT. 31 - 11:29 AM | New Jersey Governor Chris Christie tours William Street in the Old Bridge section of Sayreville after surging flood waters destroyed a number of homes in the area as a result of the high winds and rains brought by superstorm Sandy. PHOTO BY MARK R. SULLIVAN

FAR RIGHT | OCT. 31 - 12:19 PM | Work crews try to clear sand from Route 35, Ortley Beach. PHOTO BY DOUG HOOD

OCT. 31 - 1:41 PM | A damaged house in the Holgate section of Long Beach Township. PHOTO BY ROBERT WARD

ABOVE | OCT. 31 - 12:38 PM | John Murray, of Brick, and Kathleen Ficuciello, of Belmar, leave their gas cans on the hood and roof of their Jeep after waiting three hours for gasoline at the Monmouth Service Area rest stop on the Garden State Parkway in Wall after gas pumps were reopened following Sandy. PHOTO BY MARY FRANK

LEFT | OCT. 31 - 12:55 PM | Motorists wait in line at the Monmouth Service Area rest stop on the Garden State Parkway. PHOTO BY MARY FRANK

OCT. 31 | A car covered in the sand in Holgate, a section of Long Beach Township. PHOTO BY ROBERT WARD

ABOVE | OCT. 31 | Damage in Ortley Beach. PHOTO BY DOUG HOOD

LEFT | OCT. 31 | A truck pushed through the garage of a home in the Holgate section of Long Beach Township. PHOTO BY ROBERT WARD

ABOVE | OCT. 31 - 12:50 PM | Destruction at Funtown Pier following Sandy. PHOTO BY DOUG HOOD

LEFT | OCT. 31 - 1:12 PM | A roller coaster ride sits in the ocean where Casino Pier was prior to the storm. PHOTO BY DOUG HOOD

FAR LEFT | OCT. 31 - 2:51 PM | The roller coaster in Seaside Heights sits in the ocean next to the destroyed pier. PHOTO BY PETER ACKERMAN

OCT. 31 - 2:56 PM | Homes in South Mantoloking, in Brick, still burn on Wednesday afternoon.

PHOTO BY PETER ACKERMAN

OCT. 31 - 2:57 PM | Boats lay helter skelter on top of each other in a marina just south of the Mantoloking Bridge in Mantoloking. PHOTO BY PETER ACKERMAN

OCT. 31 - 3:00 PM | Mantoloking, where it was breached by the ocean in two places. PHOTO BY PETER ACKERMAN

OCT. 31 - 3:09 PM | Cots fill the floor at Monmouth University's MAC gym. This was one of Monmouth County's shelters in the wake of superstorm Sandy. PHOTO BY TOM COSTELLO

OCT. 31 - 3:10 PM | Northern Ocean County beachfront homes damaged by Sandy. PHOTO BY PETER ACKERMAN

OCT. 31 - 3:40 PM | Boats tossed by Sandy on the northern Monmouth County shoreline.

PHOTO BY PETER ACKERMAN

ABOVE | OCT. 31 - 3:42 PM | Sea Bright in northern Monmouth County. PHOTO BY PETER ACKERMAN

LEFT | OCT. 31 - 3:43 PM | Aerial view of the aftermath from Sandy in Monmouth County. PHOTO BY PETER ACKERMAN

FAR LEFT | OCT. 31 - 3:28 PM | A large section of the roof of the Great Auditorium in Ocean Grove was ripped off by the winds of superstorm Sandy. PHOTO BY PETER ACKERMAN

OCT. 31 - 4:04 PM | Homes in Union Beach destroyed by superstorm Sandy. PHOTO BY PETER ACKERMAN

OCT. 31 - 4:37 PM | Carly Litwinski, 13, of Union Beach, sits on a cot in the shelter at Monmouth University's Boylan Gym. Her family was evacuated before the storm hit. PHOTO BY TOM COSTELLO

NOV. 1 - 10:41 AM | Residents along Weber Avenue in Sayreville faced with the task of trying to rebuild their lives after flood waters from the Raritan River wiped out most of their belongings. Jeans hang out to dry on a clothing line in the backyard of 151 MacArthur Avenue. The dark line on the white fence behind the clothing is the waterline, showing how high the tidal surge was from superstorm Sandy. **PHOTO BY MARK R. SULLIVAN**

NOV. 1 - 11:08 AM | Home owner Sal Filannino, of 47 Weber Avenue in Sayreville, looks over the rubble of the interior of his home after raging flood waters filled the first floor. A 20-year resident, Filannino has endured four floods at this home. PHOTO BY MARK R. SULLIVAN

NOV. 1 - 11:26 AM | Boats pushed by flood waters onto the railroad tracks over the Manasquan River by superstorm Sandy block the rail service to points north. PHOTO BY TOM SPADER

NOV. 1 - 11:52 AM | Devastation on Brook Avenue in Union Beach. PHOTO BY TANYA BREEN

ABOVE | NOV. 1 - 12:01 PM | Debbie and Ron Krauss stand in front of their Brook Avenue home and Mustang car, which were destroyed during Sandy, in Union Beach. PHOTO BY TANYA BREEN

LEFT | NOV. 1 - 12:31 PM | Paula Harrigfeld describes the damage to her home which overlooks the mouth of the Toms River at Barnegat Bay. Her two sons Shane, 13, and James, 18, stand behind her. PHOTO BY DOUG HOOD

FAR LEFT | NOV. 1 - 12:08 PM | Devastation on Brook Avenue in Union Beach. PHOTO BY TANYA BREEN

ABOVE | NOV. 1 - 12:36 PM | James Harrigfeld, 18, starts the process of cleaning up his house. PHOTO BY DOUG HOOD

RIGHT | NOV. 1 - 12:39 PM | Margaret Knichel, of Union Beach, looks for any of her son, Shawn Knichel's, personal belongings near his Brook Avenue home, which was destroyed during Sandy. She holds up a photograph of her son and his wife, which was found in the area. PHOTO BY TANYA BREEN

FAR RIGHT | NOV. 1 - 12:25 PM | Jack and Colleen Feeney, of 725 Brook Avenue in Union Beach, sit on the front steps of what was their home, which was destroyed during Sandy.
PHOTO BY TANYA BREEN

NOV. 1 - 12:40 PM | Troy Matikonis, of South Amboy, walks past a beached sailboat with his wife Karen and four-year-old daughter Paige. PHOTO BY JASON TOWLEN

NOV. 1 - 12:55 PM | Rebecca O'Neill, of Prospect Avenue in Union Beach, looks at Sandy's destruction in her backyard. Her pool is completely covered in rubble from surrounding homes. PHOTO BY TANYA BREEN

ABOVE | NOV. 1 - 1:25 PM | South Amboy resident George Forrer surveys the damage to his Cadillac, which floated from his driveway to the backyard of his Rosewell Street home during the Sandy storm surge. PHOTO BY JASON TOWLEN

RIGHT | NOV. 1 - 1:21 PM | A Front Street home sheared in half in Union Beach. PHOTO BY TANYA BREEN

NOV. 1 - 1:30 PM | Mangled boardwalk and destroyed businesses along the beachfront resort town of Point Pleasant Beach. **PHOTO BY TOM SPADER**

ABOVE | NOV. 1 - 1:25 PM | Sea Bright Mayor, Dina Long, addresses Sea Bright residents and business owners during a town hall meeting at Rumson-Fair Haven High School to inform them it will be 7-10 days before they'll be able to return to their homes and businesses. PHOTO BY MARY FRANK

LEFT | NOV. 1 - 1:42 PM | Sea Bright resident Karen Finkelstein, listens as Sea Bright officials hold a town hall meeting at Rumson-Fair Haven High School. PHOTO BY MARY FRANK

NOV. 1 - 1:28 PM | Sea Bright officials hold a town hall meeting at Rumson-Fair Haven High School.

ABOVE | NOV. 1 - 1:21 PM | Attendees console each other as Sea Bright officials hold a town hall meeting at Rumson-Fair Haven High School. PHOTO BY MARY FRANK

LEFT | NOV. 1 - 1:47 PM | Sea Bright residents and business owners listen as Sea Bright officials hold a town hall meeting at Rumson-Fair Haven High School. PHOTO BY MARY FRANK

NOV. 1 - 2:15 PM | Angela Spruiel, of Keyport, forced out of her 1st Avenue apartment due to Sandy, spends the day at the temporary shelter at Keyport Central School. PHOTO BY TANYA BREEN

NOV. 1 | Kevin Hunter (center), of Asbury Park, and Joe Yachinski, of Lakewood, toss food items removed from the Stop & Shop on Bridge Avenue in Point Pleasant, into a garbage truck. All the contents of the store needed to be discarded after the store was flooded. PHOTO BY TOM COSTELLO

NOV. 1 - 2:28 PM | Large sections of the Point Pleasant Beach's boardwalk are missing or destroyed after superstorm Sandy. **PHOTO BY TOM SPADER**

NOV. 2 - 11:16 AM | Ray Scribner, of Paradise Park, a mobile home community in Highlands, returns to his devastated trailer to search for personal belongings. His cat, Tan, was found safe. PHOTO BY TANYA BREEN

NOV. 2 – 11:42 AM | Dale Parsons Jr. (top right in blue sweatshirt) helps and oversees the removal of breeding tanks from the Parsons Seafood Hatchery at the end of Green Street in Tuckerton.

PHOTO BY PETER ACKERMAN

NOV. 2 - 12:28 PM | A sign on the front of George Bonilla's Front Street home in Perth Amboy reads "We Survived Sandy God Bless America." Bonilla's home was badly damaged during the storm, and badly looted the following night. PHOTO BY JASON TOWLEN

ABOVE | NOV. 2 - 1:14 PM | Raritan Bay Yacht Club member Alan Uminski, of Raritan, surveys the wreckage of his 29-foot sailboat "Dilligaff" in Perth Amboy. PHOTO BY JASON TOWLEN

LEFT | NOV. 2 - 12:49 PM | Atilla Pak shovels mud from the first floor of his Perth Amboy home. PHOTO BY JASON TOWLEN

FAR LEFT | NOV. 2 - 12:36 PM | A fishing boat came to rest in the middle of Front Street in Perth Amboy. PHOTO BY JASON TOWLEN

NOV. 2 - 1:49 PM | Claims adjusters inspect and photograph the damage to the home of Sebastian Lagerveld in Point Pleasant. The home was severely damaged when a large tree crashed down on it during the storm. PHOTO BY BOB BIELK

ABOVE | NOV. 3 - 11:22 AM | Workers from the Monmouth County Department of Public Works start the huge task of cleaning up sand and debris along the shore town of Spring Lake. Here a worker throws debris toward a huge dumpster along Ocean Avenue. PHOTO BY MARK R. SULLIVAN

LEFT | NOV. 2 - 4:40 PM | At Rumson Exxon, located along River Road in Rumson, despite having no power, they decided to hand crank the gasoline from the underground tanks to the waiting customers in line. Employees Greg Fullman and Townsend Newman spin the hand cranks to fill containers full with gas. PHOTO BY MARK R. SULLIVAN

BELOW | NOV. 3 - 12:40 PM | Clean up of sand and debris along the shore town of Spring Lake begins. PHOTO BY MARK R. SULLIVAN

NOV. 3 - 1:15 PM | The homes on Long Beach Island behind the newly built up dune provided by beach replenishment fared well in superstorm Sandy, but the new dune itself was cut in half by the rough surf. The drop off from the new dune to the remaining beach is four or five feet in many places. PHOTO BY PETER ACKERMAN

ABOVE | NOV. 4 - 10:28 AM | People walk the beach in Manasquan as calm seas contrast the havoc they wreaked on homes in Manasquan during Sandy. PHOTO BY MARY FRANK

LEFT | NOV. 4 - 10:47 AM | James Grieb, 16, of Manasquan, climbs into a window on the second floor of a home on First Avenue in Manasquan, that his sister Heather rents, as she looks on from below. The landlord, Diane and Rob Johnson, of Spring Lake, left and right, stand by, as homeowners were allowed back to their homes. PHOTO BY MARY FRANK

BELOW | NOV. 4 - 4:10 PM | A sign outside Janine Miller's home on Philadelphia Avenue in Point Pleasant Beach, amidst debris removed from inside. PHOTO BY TOM COSTELLO

NOV. 4 - 11:13 AM | Shore Vineyard Church associate pastor Greg Maciunski hugs Susan Rapp-Hoppe during Sunday morning's service at the South Toms River church. The church was heavily damaged by the floodwaters, but the community came together to make emergency repairs. Rapp-Hoppe's home in Toms River was heavily damaged. PHOTO BY TOM COSTELLO

NOV. 4 - 11:23 AM | Kathleen Van Norman, of Brick, holds her 7-year-old son, Nate, during Sunday Mass at the Church of Saint Rose. PHOTO BY JASON TOWLEN

ABOVE | NOV. 4 | Janine Miller and her son Zakk stand outside her Philadelphia Avenue home in Point Pleasant Beach amidst superstrom Sandy debris removed from inside. PHOTO BY TOM COSTELLO

LEFT | NOV. 4 - 11:42 AM | Parishioners hold hands during Sunday Mass at the Church of Saint Rose in Belmar. PHOTO BY JASON TOWLEN

FAR LEFT | NOV. 4 - 11:38 AM | Cindy Cama of Belmar, center, and Bea Dunn of Shark River Hills, right, are among the parishioners packed into Sunday Mass at the Church of Saint Rose. PHOTO BY JASON TOWLEN

NOV. 5 - 10:29 AM | Denise Near, of Beach Haven, and her daughter Lauren Mennen, of Stafford, wear masks to keep the smell away as they clean out their home on South Bay Avenue in Beach Haven.

PHOTO BY PETER ACKERMAN

NOV. 5 - 11:16 AM | People at a shelter at the Toms River High School East talk about their experiences during Sandy. Marge Dowling, 97, evacuated from her Lavallette home, is going to live with her daughter in New York. PHOTO BY BOB BIELK

ABOVE | NOV. 5 - 11:35 AM | Joseph and Elvera Falduto, whose home in Toms River was flooded during the storm, at the Toms River High School East shelter. PHOTO BY BOB BIELK

RIGHT | NOV. 5 - 11:18 AM | Larry Sitkowski, of Lavallette, at the Toms River High School East shelter with his dog Sandy. PHOTO BY BOB BIELK

BELOW | NOV. 5 - 1:13 PM | Karen Pethybridge looks back at her wedding photo as she sorts through the wet mess that is her garage storage area of her Surf City home. Pethybridge sorted through each box, deciding what was worth keeping and drying out and what should be left on the curb side.

PHOTO BY PETER ACKERMAN

NOV. 5 - 1:13 PM | Residents tour the devastation of Mantoloking while traveling on a truck brought in by the National Guard. PHOTO BY DOUG HOOD

NOV. 5 - 1:31 PM | National Guard roadblock set up at the south end of Mantoloking where Route 35 merges back to a two-lane road, looking south into Brick Township. PHOTO BY DOUG HOOD

NOV. 5 - 1:34 PM | The devastation in Mantoloking as viewed by residents touring the area on a truck brought in by the National Guard. PHOTO BY DOUG HOOD

NOV. 5 - 2:07 PM | Denise Boughton and Chris Nelson, both residents of Mantoloking, react to the devastation of their town as they ride along Ocean Boulevard on a truck brought in by the National Guard.

NOV. 5 - 2:11 PM | A view of the newly-constructed Mantoloking Bridge looking back toward the mainland from the area that was washed away. PHOTO BY DOUG HOOD

OPPOSITE | NOV. 5 - 1:41 PM | Governor Chris Christie with Keansburg Mayor George Hoff and his son Shea, 10, during a visit to the Bolger Middle School in Keansburg. The governor was there to visit the volunteers and families affected by the storm. PHOTO BY ROBERT WARD

LEFT | NOV. 5 - 2:59 PM | Some of the devastation that greeted residents and business owners of North Sea Bright when they were allowed to return to their homes. PHOTO BY MARY FRANK

BOTTOM LEFT | NOV. 5 - 3:27 PM | Residents and business owners of Sea Bright are allowed to return to their homes. PHOTO BY MARY FRANK

BOTTOM RIGHT | NOV. 5 - 4:01 PM | Lt. Tracie Asbill, a United States Public Health Services nurse from Tahlequah, Oklahoma, speaks with patient Diane Olsen, of Port Reading, at a shelter in the Middlesex County College Physical Education Center. PHOTO BY JASON TOWLEN

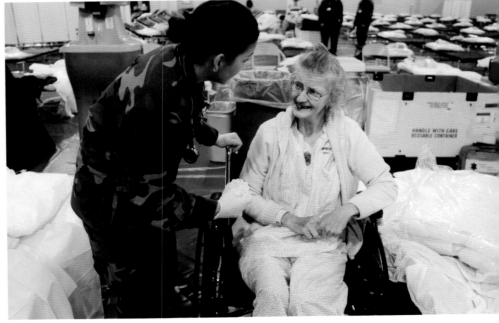

ABOVE | NOV. 5 - 4:15 PM | A long-time staple to Sea Bright, Donovan's Reef on Ocean Avenue, was reduced to mostly timber. PHOTO BY MARY FRANK

LEFT | NOV. 5 - 4:02 PM | Backyards of residences in the Tradewinds Development in Sea Bright sustained at least ten feet of property loss after superstorm Sandy slammed the Jersey Shore. PHOTO BY MARY FRANK

NOV. 6 - 12:20 PM | Michael McDonald, of Union Beach, walks through what was the dining room of his 814 Brook Avenue home. McDonald escaped his home during the tidal surge from Sandy wearing his wet suit and riding his boogie board through the window of his dining room. **PHOTO BY TANYA BREEN**

NOV. 6 - 2:13 PM | New York Giants football player Prince Amukamara poses for a picture for Nia Patrick, 4, of Seaside Heights, at the shelter at Toms River East High School. Patrick, along with her brother Kai and their grandmother Lisa Tutela were all evacuated from the barrier island during superstorm Sandy. PHOTO BY MARK R. SULLIVAN

NOV. 7 - 5:00 PM | Worker Ken MacLennan, of Hampton, carries out cabinets and other wrecked items to a pile outside of a house on Paul Boulevard in Stafford. **PHOTO BY PETER ACKERMAN**

NOV. 8 - 11:06 AM | Carolyn Gursky, of 210 Pine Street in Union Beach, talks about the volunteer work
Christian Aid Ministries has been doing to her flooded home. Christian Aid Ministries offers free cleanup
to residents in Port Monmouth and Union Beach affected by Sandy. PHOTO BY TANYA BREEN

NOV. 8 - 11:09 AM | Mary Beth Miller, of Mifflinburg, Pennsylvania, a volunteer with Christian Aid Ministries, breaks apart the flooded walls and floors of Carolyn Gursky's 210 Pine Street home with fellow volunteers. PHOTO BY TANYA BREEN

NOV. 8 - 11:56 AM | Victoria Mackies helps to clean out a storage garage at Stan's Marina in Waretown as the business tries to recover from the damage of superstorm Sandy and the Nor'easter that followed it.

PHOTO BY PETER ACKERMAN

ABOVE | NOV. 8 - 1:17 PM | The Clam Hut next to Marina on the Bay in Highlands ended up inside the marina after Sandy.
PHOTO BY BOB BIELK

RIGHT | NOV. 8 - 1:15 PM | Boats in Marina on the Bay in Highlands were tossed around and sunk during the storm. PHOTO BY BOB BIELK

OPPOSITE | NOV. 8 - 1:45 PM | Another view of the damage at Marina on the Bay in Highlands. PHOTO BY BOB BIELK

NOV. 8 - 1:50 PM | Left to right, Robert Sanfilippo, 3, Theresa Sadler, 42, Cameron Sanfilippo, 2, Diana Sanfilippo, 40, Kaylyn Hurlburt, 18 and Joel Wilson Sadler, 14, along with two others lived in a five bedroom house in Union Beach, which was destroyed by superstorm Sandy. They have been staying at a friend's two-bedroom home in Hazlet, but the friends are coming home and this family of eight has no place to go. **PHOTO BY TOM SPADER**

ABOVE | NOV. 8 - 4:45 PM | Toms River Police Chief Michael Mastronardy recovers a menorah from a 3rd Avenue home that was destroyed in Ortley Beach.
PHOTO BY TOM COSTELLO

LEFT | NOV. 8 - 2:24 PM | Billie Lambert, a volunteer with the Humane Society, from St. Petersburg, Florida, tries to feed a three-week-old kitten that got separated from her mother in the storm. A temporary emergency animal shelter was setup by the Humane Society of the United States on Collinstown Road in Barnegat. The shelter is housing stray and abandoned animals, as well as pets that were left behind by people as they evacuated. PHOTO BY PETER ACKERMAN

BELOW | NOV. 8 - 4:09 PM | Superstorm Sandy destruction along Ocean Avenue in Ortley Beach. PHOTO BY TOM COSTELLO

ABOVE | NOV. 8 - 5:51 PM | Homes destoyed near Ocean Avenue in Ortley Beach. **PHOTO BY TOM COSTELLO**

RIGHT | NOV. 8 - 5:50 PM | Homes along Ocean Avenue in Ortley Beach. **PHOTO BY TOM COSTELLO**

BELOW | NOV. 9 - 10:40 AM | An increasing number of pets and strays arrive at the Monmouth County SPCA. This seven-week-old kitten is a refugee of superstorm Sandy. **PHOTO BY TOM SPADER**

NOV. 9 - 11:00 AM | Residents of the barrier island of Long Beach Island, located in Ocean County, were allowed to re-enter the island for the first time to see their homes after the storm cut the island off from the mainland. Here, 80-year-old Elizabeth Spillane looks out from what used to be her living room, which is now open on two sides after tidal surge washed the front and one side of the home away. PHOTO BY MARK R. SULLIVAN

NOV. 9 - 11:21 AM | Vincent Renz, of Cedar Knolls, crawls out from under his vacation home on Long Beach Island, which is twisted and tilted to one side after a tidal surge moved the home from its foundation. PHOTO BY MARK R. SULLIVAN

NOV. 9 - 11:29 AM | Laurie Molinaro, a year-round Seaside Heights Sherman Avenue resident, arrives to the barrier island by bus with other property owners and residents to collect necessities. She collects her 9-year-old daughter Christina's dolls and her photograph from her bedroom. PHOTO BY TANYA BREEN

NOV. 9 - 12:30 PM | Property owner Toni Giordano hugs her tenant, Colleen Kamil, and cries as she looks around the bottom-floor apartment of her property at 220 Blaine Avenue in Seaside Heights. Giordano says the property has been in the family for 45 years. PHOTO BY TANYA BREEN

NOV. 9 - 2:16 PM | A view of the Spring Lake boardwalk looking south from the pool pavilion. New Jersey Governor Chris Christie visited here while touring Sandy damage along the Jersey Shore. PHOTO BY TOM COSTELLO

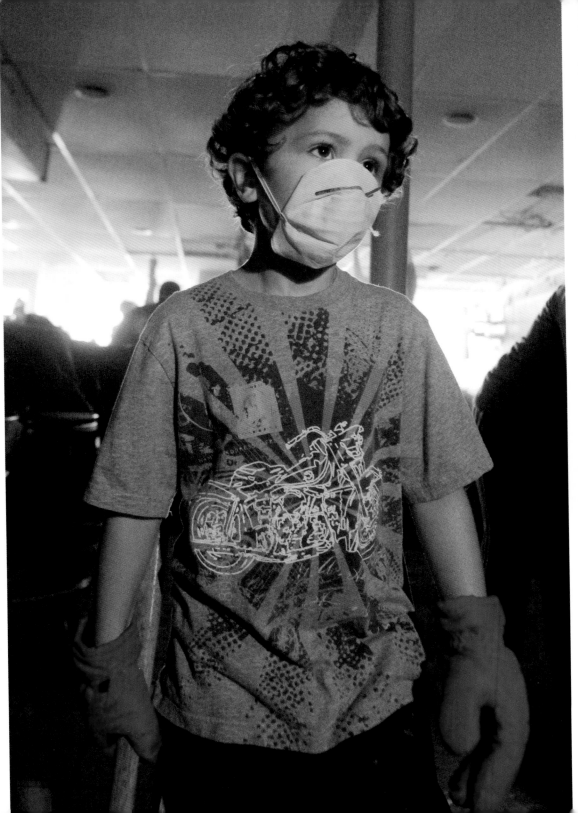

ABOVE | NOV. 10 - 12:07 PM | Rene Scott, of Little Silver, a volunteer with the Surfrider Foundation, helps clean and repair the Mayfair Hotel on Ocean Avenue in Belmar. PHOTO BY TOM SPADER

LEFT | NOV. 10 - 11:15 AM | Elliot Morris, 5, of Hamilton, a volunteer with the Surfrider Foundation appears dazed as he helps clean and repair the Mayfair Hotel. PHOTO BY TOM SPADER

OPPOSITE NOV. 10 - 11:36 AM | Reid Stoveken, 5, of Summit, a volunteer with the Surfrider Foundation, helps clean and repair the Mayfair Hotel. PHOTO BY TOM SPADER

NOV. 10 - 2:59 PM | A sad Sandy Gingras takes a moment's break as she and her helpers clean out her Beach Haven "How To Live" store, which sold many types of shore-themed lifestyle items.

PHOTO BY PETER ACKERMAN

NOV. 10 - 3:50 PM | John Scully checks out his large American Flag he was drying on his side fence while cleaning out his garage along Long Beach Boulevard in the township. PHOTO BY PETER ACKERMAN

ABOVE | NOV. 11 - 1:41 PM | Damage to a home in the Silverton section of Toms River. PHOTO BY ROBERT WARD

RIGHT | NOV. 11 - 1:41 PM | Mark Ciullo, 62, of Toms River, checks out his house on Bay Breeze Drive in Toms River. The house sustained major flood damage from superstorm Sandy. PHOTO BY ROBERT WARD

NOV. 12 - 10:33 AM | Susanne Bannon, of Union Beach, stands where her townhouse at 2 Vista Shores Drive stood before superstorm Sandy. **PHOTO BY TANYA BREEN**

NOV. 12 - 11:31 AM | Volunteer Jennifer Zappola hugs flood victim Dorris Emmons at an emergency assistance center located on Cheesequake Road in Sayreville. **PHOTO BY JASON TOWLEN**

Don't be misled by our smiling faces! This was an experience we'll never forget!
Pat Brune

ABOVE | NOV. 12 - 2:38 PM | Chris Hilly, of Ortley Beach, looks at large boats overturned in the Chadwick Island Marina. PHOTO BY BOB BIELK

LEFT | NOV. 13 - 12:28 PM | Andrew and Anita Gatto shed tears as they say goodbye to volunteers from Christ In Action who helped clean out their Beach Haven West home after flooding. PHOTO BY PETER ACKERMAN

OPPOSITE | NOV. 12 - 2:34 PM | Robert and Patricia Brune, residents of Chadwick Beach, Toms River, leave on a school bus with small suitcases of their belongings after returning to their homes for the first time after Sandy. PHOTO BY BOB BIELK

ABOVE | NOV. 14 - 11:19 AM | Superstorm Sandy and Winter Storm Athena left a twisted boardwalk along Asbury Park. PHOTO BY MARY FRANK

LEFT | NOV. 14 - 11:24 AM | Broken sections along the boardwalk in Asbury Park. PHOTO BY MARY FRANK

OPPOSITE | NOV. 14 - 1:08 PM | Mark and Kathy Rossi take a break from wheeling their wreckage out to the street with a Radio Flyer wagon to look at the damage in their neighborhood all around them on East Railway Avenue, Ortley Beach. PHOTO BY PETER ACKERMAN

RIGHT | NOV. 14 - 1:26 PM | Costume animal heads sit among the garbage thrown out on Sixth Avenue in Ortley Beach. PHOTO BY PETER ACKERMAN

FAR RIGHT | NOV. 14 - 1:36 PM | Kathy Krieger tries to remove a full garbage bag to start another as she cleans up her home on East Pennsylvania Avenue with the help of her brother, Bill Krieger, who lives on the other side of Route 35 south and still can't get into his home. PHOTO BY PETER ACKERMAN

DIG IN DEEPER

Now that you've seen Sandy's impact on the Jersey Shore in the days immediately following the storm in this book, dig in deeper:

NEWS

Stay up to date on news related to Sandy from The Asbury Park Press at

app.com/sandy

CONTRIBUTE PHOTOS

Submit your photos on Sandy during the storm and the recovery effort at

sandy.capturejerseyshore.com

DONATE

Donate to help disaster relief with the American Red Cross Jersey Coast Chapter at

redcross.org/nj/tinton-falls

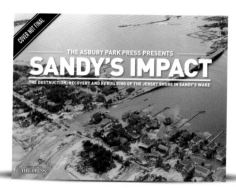

BUY

Order our second Sandy book, a hardcover edition that features in-depth articles and detailed coverage of the recovery effort at

SuperSandy.TheStormBook.com